Europe May 1941

Helsinki
Talinn
Leningrad
Riga
Moscow
Vilnius
Minsk
Warsaw
Kiev
Stalingrad
Budapest
Belgrade
Bucharest
Sofia
Tirana
Istanbul
BLACK SEA
CASPIAN SEA
Tblisi
Baku
Athens
Cyprus
Damascus
Tehran

Series 117

This is a Ladybird Expert book, one of a series of titles for an adult readership. Written by some of the leading lights and outstanding communicators in their fields and published by one of the most trusted and well-loved names in books, the Ladybird Expert series provides clear, accessible and authoritative introductions, informed by expert opinion, to key subjects drawn from science, history and culture.

The Publisher would like to thank the following for the illustrative references for this book:
Page 33: Getty Images/Tass

Every effort has been made to ensure images are correctly attributed, however if any omission or error
has been made please notify the Publisher for correction in future editions.

MICHAEL JOSEPH

UK | USA | Canada | Ireland | Australia
India | New Zealand | South Africa

Michael Joseph is part of the Penguin Random House group of companies
whose addresses can be found at global.penguinrandomhouse.com

Penguin
Random House
UK

First published 2018

001

Text copyright © James Holland, 2018

All images copyright © Ladybird Books Ltd, 2018

The moral right of the author has been asserted

Printed in Italy by L.E.G.O. S.p.A.

A CIP catalogue record for this book is available from the British Library

ISBN: 978–0–718–18651–7

www.greenpenguin.co.uk

MIX
Paper from
responsible sources
FSC® C018179

Penguin Random House is committed to a
sustainable future for our business, our readers
and our planet. This book is made from Forest
Stewardship Council® certified paper.

The Eastern Front 1941–1943

James Holland

with illustrations by
Keith Burns

Ladybird Books Ltd, London

Operation BARBAROSSA was launched early on 22 June 1941, just a few weeks after the invasion of Crete, and was the largest clash of arms the world had ever seen. Germany had amassed more than 3 million men, a colossal number, yet in truth Adolf Hitler's forces were not really ready for a campaign on this scale. Hitler had originally intended to invade the Soviet Union once France and Britain had been defeated and Europe subjugated; as a veteran of the defeat of the First World War, he understood the danger of fighting on two fronts and overstretching Germany's meagre resources.

Yet Britain had not been defeated, and hovering in the background was the United States, with its huge economic potential and open hostility to Nazi Germany. Already Germany was running short of vital supplies, but especially food and oil, and plundering the Soviet Union now seemed the best chance of making up these shortfalls. Hitler was confident of success – after all, Germany had recently defeated mighty France in six weeks, while the Red Army had been given a bloody nose by lowly Finland during what was known as the 'Winter War' of 1939–40.

The trouble was, the Soviet Union was more than ten times the size of France and the Low Countries, and Germany had a force that was only slightly larger than that of the previous year when Hitler attacked in the west. What's more, he had only 30 per cent more panzer forces, the German elite units that had been the spearhead of victory in France. As in France, most German troops were to advance into Russia on foot and by horse. The difference was that the attack front for BARBAROSSA was some 1,200 miles long.

German troops advance into the Soviet Union on 22 June 1941.

Nothing less than complete annihilation of the Red Army would do, and really this had to be achieved within 500 miles – the effective range within which the Germans could operate with the kind of speed and weight of force needed before their supply lines became over-extended and their advance ground to a halt. This was a tall order even for an army full of confidence and flushed with victory. The invasion was also to be conducted with brutal violence. 'The upcoming campaign,' Hitler told his commanders, 'is more than a mere contest of arms. It will be a struggle between two world views.'

The General Staff of the Wehrmacht – the German armed services – had already put together a plan to take the farmlands of the Ukraine. This would mean starving some 20–30 million Soviet citizens, but Nazi Germany viewed it as a war of survival so this was considered regrettably acceptable. The Soviet leadership and intelligentsia were also to be exterminated. Hitler told his generals they had three months to win this victory, after which they would then turn back west and deal with Britain once and for all.

To begin with, all seemed to go spectacularly well, helped by the Soviet leader Joseph Stalin's curious refusal to accept any warning sign of an imminent attack – and despite massive German build-up along the border in former Poland. In fact, BARBAROSSA had been the world's worst-kept secret.

Overwhelming force along what was initially a 500-mile front gouged out huge chunks of Soviet territory in the first fortnight of battle as the German armies swept forward, while above, the Luftwaffe hammered the Red Army's air forces. The Baltic States were swiftly overrun in the north, while in the centre much of former Poland was swept aside. Once again, the German armies seemed unstoppable.

Operation BARBAROSSA
22 June–25 August 1941

400 km

0   250 miles

Stalin appeared to have been briefly frozen with panic but quickly recovered. On 30 June he formed a war cabinet, the People's Commissariat of Defence (GKO), and the next day spoke to the people, appealing to their patriotism. At the same time, the security services were united under the People's Commissariat for Internal Affairs (NKVD) and ordered to clamp down even harder on defeatism and deserters, and to ensure there was no slackening of the struggle for survival.

Meanwhile, Hitler now began meddling in military matters despite having no qualifications for such high-level interference. On 19 July, he ordered that Leningrad in the north and the Ukraine in the south were the priorities and that his two precious panzer groups, currently pushing towards Moscow, should be sent to help with these drives once Smolensk, 360 miles south-west of the capital, had been crushed. The Soviet capital would be left to the Luftwaffe even though there were nothing like enough bombers to do the job.

Four days later, he changed his orders again, now demanding that the Luftwaffe support the southern drive and also the Finns, who were advancing against Leningrad in the north. He thought this would deter the British from intervening in the Arctic. At the time there was no possible way in which Britain could mount such an operation, something that was glaringly obvious to anyone with a basic knowledge of planning. Moscow was barely bombed at all.

Another directive was issued on 30 July and yet another on 12 August as Hitler obsessed over his flanks and the slowing up of their advance. By this time, the Red Army was starting to regain its balance, while the Germans were reaching the limits of their lines of supply.

German Heinkel 111 bombers attack Moscow.

Günther Sack was a young anti-aircraft gunner attached to the German 9th Division in Army Group South in the Ukraine. In the second week of July his team suffered a puncture on their gun carriage, which held them up, then on 15 July their truck broke down with a seized engine. Then the trailer broke again, so that it wasn't until the end of July that they finally caught up with the rest of the division. His and his crew's experience was a common one.

Meanwhile, a further 5 million men had been called up to the Red Army. The Soviets had been horrifically mauled in the opening stages of BARBAROSSA but they had not been completely defeated. Far from it. 'We very soon had to accustom ourselves,' wrote Hans von Luck, an officer in the 7th Panzer Division, 'to her almost inexhaustible masses of land forces, tanks, and artillery.'

The German advance was once again increasingly dependent on her railway network, but the Soviet Union operated on a different gauge. This meant changing the tracks as they moved east, because Stalin had also ordered a scorched earth policy as the Red Army fell back. All factories, bridges, farmland and infrastructure were to be destroyed so the Germans could not use it. On 24 June, Stalin had also ordered the establishment of a Soviet – or council – for Evacuation. The vast bulk of the USSR's industry was to be moved lock, stock and barrel to the Urals, some 600 miles east of Moscow. By the beginning of August this was already well under way.

The Germans continued to win victories – and capture more prisoners than they could cope with. This meant many Soviet POWs soon starved to death, as there was already a shortage of food for the German troops without having to feed many more prisoners than they had expected. Word of the poor treatment of prisoners soon spread, and increasing numbers of Soviet soldiers now evaded capture and began to organize themselves to operate behind the lines as partisans. This further hindered the German supply lines to the front.

The Black Sea port of Kiev in the south was captured by the Germans on 19 August. It was another massive victory – but not massive enough. Hitler now agreed that the main effort should be focused on Moscow, but this involved an enormous redeployment of forces, which took time – too much time, and a precious resource of which they were running short. Operation TYPHOON was launched on 30 September, three and a half months after the invasion had begun. And by this time, it had begun to rain.

Another 750,000 Soviet men were captured, but Moscow was still a long way off and the rain soon turned the rough roads to mud. Vehicles increasingly broke down or became stuck. Fuel could no longer be supplied in the quantities required. Casualties were mounting and manpower was running short. Replacements of men, machines and spare parts could not be found or delivered in the numbers needed. What made the Wehrmacht special was the speed with which it operated. But when it slowed down, it was not quite so special after all.

Soviet prisoners of war trudge into captivity.

None the less, huge swathes of territory were now in German hands. In Moscow, the Soviet leadership was struggling to control the crisis. Although the German advance was slowing, by October they were just 120 miles from the capital. Civilians were ordered to help build an extra defence line, while General Georgi Zhukov was brought in to defend the city with massive reinforcements of troops. At the same time, more industry and even state archives were sent east to the Urals.

The Germans continued to close on the city, but rain had now given way to snow and a dramatic drop in temperatures for which they were simply not equipped. Only in the Luftwaffe had anyone thought ahead and ordered winter clothing. The army had none at all. Sixty miles from Moscow, Hans von Luck faced a Soviet counter-attack with Russian troops on skis and wearing white camouflage. 'We sensed catastrophe,' he wrote, 'and thought of Napoleon's fate.' Back in 1812, Napoleon's French army had been decimated by the freezing Russian winter.

Others feared the same. Colonel Hermann Balck visited the front in November and discovered panzer divisions operating at just a tenth of their strength in both men and machines. He was deeply shaken. Fritz Todt, the Armaments Minister, was horrified to learn that German tanks and vehicles were freezing up and unable to move while Soviet tanks could still operate in the extreme cold. With unusual frankness, he told Hitler at the end of November that the war against the Soviet Union could no longer be won.

Meanwhile, despite the vast losses suffered so far, General Zhukov was preparing to defend Moscow with no fewer than 1.25 million men, 7,600 guns and nearly 1,000 tanks. What's more, an incredible 2,593 industrial operations had been relocated in the Urals since June, along with 1.5 million railway wagons and much of the Soviet industrial workforce.

German troops advanced to within 30 miles of Moscow. Stalin and the GKO still feared the worst, but by this time most of the attackers were frozen, half starving and all but broken. On the night of 4/5 December, as temperatures plummeted further to minus 35, the Red Army counter-attacked, catching their enemy completely off-guard. Suddenly it was the Germans who were on the back foot.

Six months earlier, Germany had had one enemy – Great Britain – but by the middle of December 1941 faced Britain, the Soviet Union and now the United States, following the Japanese attack on Pearl Harbor. Japan was an Axis partner and on 11 December Hitler declared war on America. By this time Nazi Germany was short of money, food, coal, oil and other vital resources necessary for war. In 1918, Germany had signed an armistice because it had run out of money and could no longer win. That moment had arrived again now, as men like Fritz Todt understood.

Hitler, however, refused to accept this and responded by sacking a number of highly experienced and brilliant commanders such as Field Marshal Heinz Guderian. He also fired the head of the army, Field Marshal Walther von Brauchitsch, and made himself Commander-in-Chief instead. This would mean more micro-managing and more rigid control. A key feature of the German Army's success had always been freedom of movement and the right of commanders to make swift, on-the-spot decisions. With Hitler directly in charge, there were now barriers to such rapid decision-making.

Moscow remained as out of reach as ever.

Meanwhile, to the north, Leningrad, Russia's second city, had been under siege since September. A major German objective, the city stood on a 30-mile-wide isthmus between the Baltic and Lake Ladoga. Finnish troops were pressing south from the north and had captured two thirds of the lake's shores, while the Germans were now within 10 miles of the city, having crossed the River Neva to the south, and had also reached the lake. The only lifeline to the city for the defenders was across the southern part of Lake Ladoga and via the railheads of the towns of Volkhov and Tikhvin on the far side.

The Germans planned to pound Leningrad into the dust with artillery and bombing. The starving civilian population would be deported east, the defending troops destroyed, and then the city would be levelled with demolition charges. There was to be no mercy.

German troops took Tikhvin on 9 November, but Leningrad was still grimly holding out. With the lake now frozen over, a passage was created across the ice from the far shore to the city; it was known as the 'Road of Life'. Even so, nothing like enough supplies were getting through. Hundreds of thousands of citizens were dying from a combination of starvation, water shortage and disease, their bodies often left where they died. The survivors were eating birds, then cats and dogs, then rats and even dead humans.

There were still large numbers of Red Army troops, however, and on 9 December, as the German attackers froze, they recaptured Tikhvin and then pushed the enemy back along a 90-mile stretch. The terrible siege, though, was still far from over.

The streets of Leningrad during the brutal siege.

'An interesting question is what are the Russians capable of doing in the spring?' noted Colonel Hermann Balck in his diary on 3 March 1942. 'One thing is clear,' he added, 'if we can grasp the initiative again, they will be finished.'

This was what worried the Soviet leadership, despite the catastrophic winter for the Germans and despite Red Army troops continuing to push German forces back along a wide front since December. Stalin and the GKO faced a tricky dilemma. Winter would soon be over and the traditional summer campaigning season would be upon them. The Germans would then, unquestionably, resume the offensive. Despite saving Moscow and holding on in Leningrad, and despite making some gains since then, the Red Army's situation remained perilous. Losses had been enormous, the relocation of war industry to the Urals had hampered the speed of production, and they were still learning lessons about how best to turn the tide against the enemy invaders. Manpower was not limitless, even in the Soviet Union. Nor could the will of the people to keep fighting be necessarily assured, despite totalitarian Communist rule. The conundrum facing the Soviet leadership was whether to go on the defensive and build up strength, or to strike first and try to upset the inevitable German offensive plans in the process.

At the urging of Marshal Semyon Timoshenko, Stalin decided to attack. A bulge in the line had been formed around the town of Izyum, south of the key city of Kharkov. By attacking north out of the salient and south from the north of Kharkov on 12 May 1942, they hoped to encircle the city and with it the German Sixth Army.

Stalin and Marshal Timoshenko.

Unfortunately for the Soviets, the Izyum offensive was a disaster, as the Germans defeated the northern thrust and severed the salient, cutting off and encircling the main Red Army assault in turn. Another 240,000 Soviet prisoners were taken, along with 1,200 tanks and 2,600 guns. For Stalin and the GKO, the disaster could scarcely have been worse. Vyacheslav Molotov, the Foreign Minister, was sent to Britain then America to plead with the Allies to launch an offensive against Germany in the west as soon as possible. The possibility of the Soviet Union being completely defeated loomed heavily for Stalin and the GKO.

Meanwhile, in the skies, Luftwaffe fighter aces continued to rule. Men like Bubi Hartmann, Gerd Barkhorn and Günther Rall were amassing hundreds of aerial victories, using their superior skill, experience and machines to blow the Soviet air forces out of the sky.

Despite this dominance, however, the problems confronting the Germans had not gone away, as the newly promoted Major-General Balck discovered when he arrived at the front to take command of 11th Panzer Division. After BARBAROSSA, 11th Panzer had been reduced to a few battered remnants and even after rebuilding over the winter was still operating at only 60 per cent strength. They were far from alone, and the enormous scale of the Eastern Front, with ongoing shortages of food, oil and just about everything else, meant that Operation BLUE, the planned German drive south to the oilfields of the Caucasus, would be launched with less than they had had the previous summer and with longer lines of communication that would only get longer. What's more, the cream of German manpower had already gone, most of her finest young men obliterated by a year of fighting in this vast, unforgiving country.

Bubi Hartmann (top), Günther Rall (left), and Gerd Barkhorn (bottom).

Nor was Operation BLUE the only German effort. Capturing Moscow had been abandoned for the time being, but Hitler had not given up hopes of taking Leningrad and General Erich von Manstein was planning to launch a renewed attack at the end of August.

The suffering of those in Leningrad is hard to comprehend. Over a million had perished since the siege had begun, but the onset of spring and then summer had seen the ice on Lake Ladoga melt. By July, over a million tons of supplies had been shipped across the lake to the city, while more than half a million civilians had been evacuated and some 310,000 troops brought in, along with large numbers of guns and ammunition.

In a striking act of defiance, it was these guns, along with those of the Soviet Baltic Fleet, that were able to silence German artillery early in August to allow the first performance in the city of Dmitri Shostakovich's newly composed Seventh Symphony, 'Leningrad'. To all those who braved going out to hear this incredible concert, the Leningrad Philharmonic played in perfect unison with the Russian guns. Miraculously, not a single German shell fell nearby. The event, broadcast around the world, was a stunning propaganda victory that struck a vital chord for Soviet patriotism.

On 19 August, the Red Army attacked from Volkhov, destroying the best part of two German divisions in the process. This time, their pre-emptive strike worked and von Manstein's offensive plans were scuppered. Leningrad also remained as tantalizingly out of reach as Moscow.

The Leningrad Philharmonic playing Shostakovich's new symphony in the ruins of the besieged city.

There was also a further operation by the Germans before Operation BLUE was launched. While most of the Crimean peninsula had been captured the previous November, the port and fortress of Sebastopol had remained besieged, stubbornly defended and supplied by the Soviet Navy, which had retained control of the Black Sea.

The Red Army had tried to relieve the city the previous Christmas by launching an amphibious assault on the Kerch peninsula further to the east, but this had been recaptured again by May 1942 and a renewed Axis assault on Sebastopol began. More units of the overstretched Luftwaffe were sent south to the Crimea, as were some 600 pieces of artillery, including two monstrous railway guns. The 'Dora' needed sixty steam engines just to move it and involved building new railway tracks, as well as tying up some 4,120 men. The shell it fired had a diameter of 80cm – almost one metre wide! Operating these two guns caused a logistical headache out of all proportion to its offensive benefits. As many as 500 men were needed just to fire it. 'An extraordinary piece of engineering,' noted General Franz Halder, Chief of Staff of the Army, 'but useless.'

Certainly the guns didn't secure a swift victory. By the end of June, Sebastopol still held out and the Germans then resorted to using poison smoke to clear the caverns below the city. Not until 9 July did the defenders finally surrender. The cost to both sides was huge, but was felt more keenly by the Germans, who had thrown an entire army into the final battle; 25,000 German soldiers died in that last offensive and 70,000 overall. Sebastopol also sucked up gargantuan amounts of resources at an average rate of 135 railway wagons a day. It was something of a Pyrrhic victory, while the grim defence did nothing but stiffen Red Army resolve.

When Operation BLUE was launched with a mighty artillery barrage at 2.15 a.m. on 28 June 1942, General Balck's 11th Panzer Division were at the front of the advance. By 9 a.m. they had crossed a vital river obstacle and, while under fire, Balck went forward to see his infantry, then accompanied his panzers as they sped forward. 'It was an intoxicating picture,' he wrote, 'the wide, treeless plains covered with 150 advancing tanks, above them a Stuka squadron.' The advance continued, but this time the enemy melted away, retreating before they could be captured. The Red Army was learning.

None the less, Operation BLUE appeared to be going well, although Hitler was beginning to micro-manage once more. From the depths of his bunker, the Wolf's Lair in East Prussia, he insisted on sending two precious panzer divisions west to France then concentrating too many others against Rostov, leaving flanks dangerously exposed. When the folly of this became apparent, he flew into a fit of rage. Nothing was ever Hitler's fault. 'The situation is getting more and more intolerable,' noted General Halder. 'This so-called leadership is characterized by a pathological reaction to the impressions of the moment and a total lack of any understanding of the command machinery and its possibilities.'

Even so, Operation BLUE had smashed the Red Army's front and thereafter the German advance into the Caucasus was rapid. Maikop, a major objective, was captured, although its oil wells had been destroyed by the retreating Russians. Meanwhile, General Friedrich Paulus's Sixth Army was also advancing east towards Stalingrad on the River Volga.

The outskirts of Stalingrad were reached on 10 August, but by then the advance south into the Caucasus was beginning to slow as once again the supply lines began to stretch and Red Army resistance grew. The Germans were now more than 500 miles further on, the distance at which they could no longer operate with the speed and manoeuvrability that was the benchmark of their operational and tactical skill. They had exceeded what is known as the culmination point.

Hitler had dreamed of creating a mammoth Axis link between Rommel's forces advancing from Egypt into the Middle East and his armies in the Soviet Union, but this was pure fantasy. In fact, it was also absurd to believe they could capture the world's third-largest producing oilfields in Baku, even though that had been the prime strategic aim of Operation BLUE.

Such ambition was extremely flawed thinking for a number of reasons. First, the Red Army would destroy the wells in advance as they had at Maikop. Second, even if they didn't, the Germans had no means of either refining the oil or, more importantly, transporting it west. The only pipelines were few and far between and all headed east to the Urals. Oil was transported around the world almost entirely by ship – as it still is today – yet Germany had neither shipping nor access to the world's oceans. The alternative was the railway, but the Reichsbahn was already operating at capacity and had nothing like enough oil wagons.

Incredibly, no one within the Reich appears to have considered any of this.

Instead, the Germans believed the Soviet Union was already on the point of collapse and that the capture of Baku would hasten its capitulation. However, because the Luftwaffe did not have the aircraft to bomb or spy on either Baku or the growing industrial relocation in the Urals, they had little idea that the Soviet Union was rapidly and very effectively increasing its armaments production. Faulty intelligence, compounded by Hitler's desire always to listen to over-optimistic appreciations, meant Operation BLUE had been launched on an entirely false promise. For example, German intelligence reckoned the Soviet Union had 6,600 aircraft when in fact they had 22,000. They thought the Red Army had 6,000 tanks when the real number was 24,446. In artillery they were even further off the mark: 7,800 guns instead of the 33,000 that was the reality. These were very big errors.

As it happened, however, the Germans never reached Baku. Once again, their armies had run out of steam.

This marked the end for General Halder, who was fired in September. Ironically, as some of Germany's best commanders were finding themselves out of a job, the Red Army had learned much after more than a year of bitter warfare and a number of their very best commanders were now coming to the fore. One of those was General Konstantin Rokossovsky, of Polish descent and a man who had been on the receiving end of Stalin's purge of the Red Army in the 1930s. Most of the army's senior leadership had been executed – one reason for poor performance early in the war – and Rokossovsky had been lucky to lose only his teeth and a number of fingernails. Since his release from prison he had repeatedly proved himself to be one of Stalin's most capable and inspirational generals and had swiftly risen up the ranks as a result. By November 1942, he was commanding the Don Front, a group of armies facing the Germans at Stalingrad – and brilliantly so too.

Marshal Konstantin Rokossovsky.

As the winter of 1942 began to bite, it was clear that Paulus's Sixth Army was becoming horribly bogged down at Stalingrad, while the El Dorado of Baku was as out of reach as ever. Either side of Sixth Army were Axis allies: one Italian army to the north and a Romanian one on each side, and their forces were neither as well equipped nor of equal fighting quality as the Germans. Their fighting capacity had been further weakened by attrition and the advent of winter.

Realizing this, on 19 November the Red Army launched Operation URANUS to the north and south of the city. Through the winter mist, Russian troops attacked in thick snow like apocalyptic spectres, smashing their way through both Romanian armies to link up 35 miles west of Stalingrad. Trapped in the middle were more than a quarter of a million troops, including the remains of Sixth Army, once one of Germany's finest. By 24 November, a massive gap had opened up between the German forces to the north and those still in the Caucasus. How the tables had turned. Paulus asked permission to try to break out, but this was refused. Instead, the Luftwaffe were ordered to fly in supplies until Sixth Army could be relieved. They never managed a fraction of what was needed.

It was Rokossovsky's Don Front that was now ordered to destroy the Germans at Stalingrad. The offensive began on 10 January 1943. On the 16th, the main airfield was captured and with that the fate of Sixth Army was sealed for good. Against Hitler's wishes, Paulus surrendered on 31 January in what was the most crushing and devastating defeat so far suffered by the Germans in the war.

With the triumph of Stalingrad, Stalin now called for a renewed Red Army drive westwards using three fronts – that is, groups of armies. Soviet industry was producing increasing amounts of war materiel and more was coming from the USA and Britain, while the Red Army was showing signs of increasing competence. The plan was still overambitious, however.

Even so, by March the Germans had been thrown back between 200 and 420 miles. The Italian, Hungarian and two Romanian armies had all been utterly destroyed, and all the ground lost in the Caucasus retaken. German forces west of Moscow had survived being encircled, but Kharkov had also been retaken – Hitler had forbidden any retreat from the city, but this time the SS Panzer Corps that held it ignored the order and pulled out on 15 February.

Despite these stunning reverses, suddenly it was the Red Army that was overstretched with lines of supply that were far too long. On 4 March, they halted their advances only for the Germans to counter-attack. Rather than allow themselves to be encircled, the Red Army sensibly fell back out of comparative danger, although it meant abandoning Kharkov yet again, as well as, some 250 miles to the north, Bryansk and Orel. The Russians did, however, hold on to the city of Kursk so that by the time the long, bloody and bitter winter fighting finally died down at the end of March there was a large bulge, or salient, sticking out some 60 miles to the west of the town and running some 150 miles north to south.

It was clear the lull was just that – a pause – and that the Germans would soon use the summer to go on the offensive once more. With the key cities of Orel and Kharkov to the north and south, it was also obvious that this large salient of rolling, well-cultivated farmland was where the next great battle would take place.

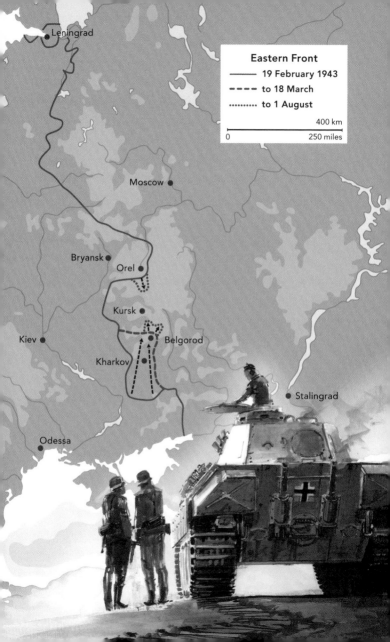

Eastern Front

— 19 February 1943
--- to 18 March
···· to 1 August

0	400 km
	250 miles

Leningrad

Moscow

Bryansk
Orel

Kursk

Kiev

Belgorod

Kharkov

Odessa

Stalingrad

For Hitler and the Nazi leadership, the war in the Soviet Union had never been just about gaining food, oil and living space. There was also an ideological element: a battle of survival in which German 'Aryans' were fighting inferior 'Slavs' or *Untermenschen* – inferior beings. For the Nazis, it was a racial war. By making it so they were rather shooting themselves in the foot, however. During the 1930s, the Ukraine had suffered a famine in which millions had died. Many Ukrainians held Stalin directly responsible and even welcomed the Nazi invaders, but although some were absorbed into the Wehrmacht, many more faced barbarity. Villages were burned, people executed, and others rounded up and taken prisoner.

Soviet prisoners of war were also treated appallingly compared with western Allied POWs. Those who did not die of starvation and illness were forced into slave labour. So began a cycle of barely comprehensible violence and cruelty.

Large numbers of Soviet civilians and former soldiers who had fled the German advances or somehow escaped their clutches had, by the spring of 1943, become particularly vicious and increasingly effective bands of outlaws, or partisans, organized from within the Soviet Union by the NKVD, the Soviet intelligence service. These partisans were blowing up railway lines and roads, attacking convoys and ambushing any troops they could, while also passing back vital intelligence. In effect, the partisans had become a fourth armed service, and made the already difficult task of supply even harder for the Germans.

For the Germans, clearing the Kursk salient was an urgent priority. The bulge added around 150 miles to the front line, which was tying up some eighteen divisions. By straightening the line, they would free up those men and, more importantly, would destroy the main concentration of Red Army forces. These now included the Central Front, which had been formed back in February and which was commanded by Rokossovsky, as well as General Nikolai Vatutin's Voronezh Front in the southern part of the salient.

Hopes for the forthcoming battle were high. It would be a chance to restore prestige and confidence and show the world the Wehrmacht was far from beaten. From April and into June 1943, the Germans began preparing for this next massive attack, codenamed CITADEL.

It was Marshal Zhukov who persuaded Stalin and the GKO to stand firm, dig in, use the increasing amounts of war materiel coming from the Urals, and make the Germans fight for every yard. Only once the German attack had been blunted would the Soviets go on the offensive. For once, Stalin listened. In April, the Red Army began digging a massive series of defences. In all, there were five 'belts' around the salient and Kursk itself, and a further three behind. Each of these belts included several lines of bunkers, gun positions, minefields and wire. The entire population was evacuated from the outer zone and villages turned into small fortresses and strongpoints. Intelligence from partisans, from British code-breakers and from Soviet spies and signals intelligence made it clear the Germans would attack from two points, one in the north and one in the south. This, then, was where the defences were made strongest.

Soviet intelligence was so good that by the beginning of July they not only knew where the Germans would attack but with what and when. On the other hand, German intelligence was also good enough to know that Rokossovsky was staying in a small cottage halfway between Kursk and the north edge of the salient, and so on the night of 3 July, two days before CITADEL's launch, two planes came over and destroyed the house. By chance, however, Rokossovsky was not there. It was a lucky escape.

The Germans had amassed some 900,000 men, 10,000 guns, 2,700 tanks and 2,000 aircraft. General Kurt Student and the men of Ninth Army would attack from the north, while General Hermann Hoth's Fourth Panzer Army assaulted from the south. Inside the salient were some 1.3 million Red Army troops, double the number of German guns and 3,600 tanks. A military rule of thumb is never to attack without at least a three-to-one advantage, but not only did the Germans not have this, they were also confronting the most formidable defences they had yet come up against. Soviet air power was also on the rise with some 2,400 bombers, fighters and ground attack aircraft such as the Ilyushin Il-2 Sturmovik.

What's more, captured prisoners had revealed that the attack would begin in the early hours of 5 July 1943. In an effort to put the enemy off their stride, Rokossovsky had opened up 500 of his own guns first at around 2.20 a.m., along with a similar number of mortars and 100 Katyusha rocket-launchers. This certainly shook German confidence, but did not stop them launching an immense artillery barrage at around 4.30 a.m. Half an hour later, the Germans attacked from the south and at 5.50 a.m. they began their assault from the north.

The Fourth Panzer Army in the south was full of tanks, motorized infantry and artillery, and included new mighty Panther and Tiger tanks. It was the kind of armoured spearhead that had cut swathes through much of Europe, but now many of the new tanks broke down, while others found themselves being pummelled in turn by Russian anti-tank guns from their well-prepared positions. In the north, similarly prepared and well-sighted positions also intercepted the main German thrust. One after another, German tanks were hit and knocked out.

By 10 July, the Germans had managed to penetrate 20 miles in the south and about 7 miles in the north, and had reached only the third line of defence. The next day, 11 July, the panzers renewed their attack from the south. The fine summer weather was breaking and by the morning of the 12th, as the panzers neared the small town of Prokhorovka, thunderclouds were building. Joined by the II SS Panzer Corps with some 600 tanks, including 100 Tigers, they were now confronted by a counter-thrust from the Fifth Guards Tank Army.

The Battle of Prokhorovka, which followed that day, has often been called the 'greatest tank battle in history'. Although the numbers involved have often been wildly exaggerated, it did involve more than 800 on both sides. The Russians came off worst and left some 400 burnt-out hulks on the field of battle, but despite this, that same day Hitler called a halt to CITADEL. Two days earlier, the Allies had landed in Sicily, requiring a diversion of resources and especially Luftwaffe aircraft to meet this new threat – one that was far closer to home.

Now came the Red Army counter-attack. Rokossovky's men, with a mass of tanks and artillery, ground down the best German efforts to hold on, gradually pushing forward. Orel was retaken on 4 August. At the same time, almost 100,000 coordinated partisans began what was known as the 'Railway War': blowing up railway lines in thousands of places, killing rail crew and paralysing the German lines of communication. On the night of 20/21 July, for example, they cut the main line from Bryansk in 430 places.

In the south, Vatutin's front was joined by another group of armies, the Steppe Front, and then Zhukov himself was sent forward to coordinate this massive combined counter-offensive there. The battered, exhausted and demoralized Germans had no answer. On 5 August, Belgorod was retaken. By midday on 23 August, Kharkov was once again in Soviet hands, and this time would remain so. In some fifty days of fighting, Red Army losses had been horrific but so had those of the Germans: some half a million dead, wounded and missing, and around thirty divisions destroyed. These were casualties they simply could not afford.

What's more, the Red Army was now a very different beast. The factories of the Urals, along with US and British convoys, were providing ever-greater firepower on the ground and in the air, while the Soviet commanders now understood the importance of the 'deep battle'. Five new tank armies were thrusting deep into the German line after any breakthrough, at great speed and with the support of large numbers of aircraft, before the enemy could pull back. It was proving very effective.

For the Soviet Union, this was the Great Patriotic War. Appealing to traditional Russian concepts of patriotism had been an effective ploy by Stalin, but the men – and women – of the Red Army were also made to keep fighting by extraordinary levels of brutality. Behind the advancing armies were NKVD troops who swept into newly retaken areas and arrested anyone suspected of collaborating with the Germans in any way whatsoever. These troops also dealt with deserters or those who made any other kind of infringement. One new lieutenant was executed at Stalingrad because several of his men had deserted before he'd even arrived at his post.

In July 1942, Stalin authorized the formation of *shtrafbats* – punishment battalions of former officers who had been demoted for perceived cowardice or lack of resolution. They were usually sent to the most difficult parts of the front. Clearing a minefield, for example, was the kind of task given to a *shtrafbat*: the men would simply be ordered to cross it until the mines had been detonated. There were also punishment companies – *shtrafroty* – made up of miscreant junior commanders. Life was very cheap in the Red Army, but especially so in these punishment units. Very few survived.

Women were also used widely from October 1941 onwards. The 'Night Witches' were an all-female night-bomber unit using old biplanes. Needless to say, casualties were high. There were also female fighter and dive-bomber units in the air force. Soviet women were used as snipers, and were often very effective too.

After Kursk, the Red Army continued to drive west into the Ukraine, using five army groups simultaneously. This autumn offensive became collectively known as the Battle of the Dnepr, the river that ran through this part of the Soviet Union. Rokossovsky's Central Front led the way, reaching the Dnepr north of Kiev in September and closely followed to the south by the Veronezh Front. Bitter fighting followed and Kiev was not retaken until 6 November, but it meant the old capital of the Ukraine was now back in Soviet hands and with it a huge bridgehead some 200 miles wide and 90 deep.

By the end of December, the entire front had shifted hundreds of miles westwards, the Crimea had been isolated, the Dnepr crossed and the Central Front had created a vast bridgehead that extended as far as the city of Karosten at the edge of the Pripyat Marshes.

The Red Army triumphed to the north as well. By January 1944, the Leningrad and Volkhov Fronts had amassed just under a million men and nearly 22,000 guns, while lying offshore was the Baltic Fleet. The Red Army attack began on 14 January and soon pushed the Germans back. The last German shell to land on Leningrad fell on 23 January and four days later, at 8 o'clock in the evening, the sky over the city lit up with a mass of colour as more than 300 guns fired a salute of triumph. After 880 days, the terrible siege of Leningrad was finally over.

There was plenty of hard fighting still to come, but no one, least of all the Germans, could now doubt the outcome.

The Soviet Union would have its revenge.

The 'Night Witches'.

Further Reading

GENERAL HISTORIES

Chris Bellamy *Absolute War: Soviet Russia in the Second World War* (Pan, 2009)

Antony Beevor *Stalingrad* (Penguin, 2007)

Svetlana Alexievich *The Unwomanly Face of War* (Penguin, 2017)

Robert M. Citino *Death of the Wehrmacht: The German Campaigns of 1942* (University Press of Kansas, 2007)

Robert M. Citino *The Wehrmacht Retreats: Fighting a Lost War, 1943* (University Press of Kansas, 2012)

Robert M. Citino *The Wehrmacht's Last Stand: The German Campaigns of 1944–1945* (University Press of Kansas, 2017)

MEMOIRS

Hermann Balck *Order in Chaos* (University Press of Kentucky, 2017)

Hans von Luck *Panzer Commander* (Cassell, 2002)

Konstantin Rokossovsky *A Soldier's Duty* (Central Books, 1985)

Erwin Bartmann *Für Volk and Führer* (Helion, 2013)

NOVELS

Helen Dunmore *The Siege* (Penguin, 2002)

Vasily Grossman *Life and Fate* (Vintage, 2006)

Guy Sajer *The Forgotten Soldier* (Cassell, 1999)